DATE LOANED

GUILDS

GUILDS
Neil Grant

Illustrated with photographs
and contemporary prints

◄—A FIRST BOOK—►

FRANKLIN WATTS, INC.
NEW YORK / 1972

(frontispiece) The large and splendid guildhall in Bruges (Belgium): a reminder of the power and pride of the guilds in a medieval city.

Cover design by Rafael Hernandez

Library of Congress Cataloging in Publication Data

Grant, Neil.
    Guilds.

    (A First book)
    SUMMARY: Traces the history of guilds from their beginnings in medieval Europe to their decline in the sixteenth century.
    Bibliography: p.
    1. Guilds–Europe–History–Juvenile literature. [1. Guilds–History] I. Title.
HD6456.G7   338.6'32'094   72-3616
ISBN 0-531-00771-5

CONTENTS

GUILDS

Craftsmen selling their wares at market stalls.

 INTRODUCTION

In old European towns, the largest building other than the church was the guildhall. Except for the very rich and the very poor, most townsmen in medieval Europe belonged to a guild. The chief merchants, shopkeepers, and craftsmen, who were the leaders of the guilds, were often members of the town councils as well. They were responsible for all the services that are carried out today by special officials or city departments, including police work, welfare, and justice.

When a member of the guild was ill, the guild provided him with food and medicine. If his home was robbed or burned, the guild helped him start afresh. When he was dying, the guild made sure that a priest visited him, and if he died poor, the guild gave him a decent funeral.

The guild helped to protect the consumer as well as the producer. It ensured a fair standard of work and punished those who produced goods of an inferior quality or who charged unfair prices. A wine seller who sold bad wine might have to drink a jugful of his own brew, and perhaps stand in the stocks where he could be pelted with garbage by the citizens he had cheated.

No one was allowed to work before dawn or after sunset because high-quality work could not be done by candlelight, and there was no other form of artificial light. As a result, men worked much longer hours during summer than they did during the winter. In fact, some guilds ruled that no work should be done at all during the month of January.

[1]

During the Middle Ages the Church taught that usury (the lending of money at interest) was a sin, and medieval people believed that it was wrong to make large profits by selling goods for much more than they cost. This rule, however, was not always obeyed, even in the Middle Ages. But a man who *did* raise his prices above the general level could be punished by the guilds.

He could also get into trouble if he reduced his prices, because others in the same business would then suffer a loss of trade, and the guilds did not favor competition. The number of workers or apprentices employed by one man was strictly regulated, and partnerships or "mergers" generally were not allowed. It was difficult, if not impossible, for a foreigner, or even a man from the next town, to set up a business. Nor could a foreign workman be hired unless all the local workmen were employed. The wages and conditions of work were also regulated by the guild.

The guild had its lighter side, and every year a feast was held in the guildhall. All the members attended with their wives, whose presence did not prevent heavy drinking and the playing of rough but cheerful games of the sort that are still played in some college fraternities. A few guilds had women members, for although most women were kept busy with domestic tasks, some did work for their living.

Many guilds also staged an annual entertainment, or pageant. It might take the form of a carnival, with men dressed in strange costumes, or it might be a simple kind of play. Usually the play represented a Bible legend that was related to the occupation of the guild members. For instance, the guild of fishmongers in a German town performed a scene from the legend of Jonah and the whale. It seemed a very suitable story for the fishmongers, because it was both religious and relevant to their work. Sometimes these entertainments were transported from town to town. The actors carried their own stage, and performed in market squares or in any convenient open space.

Although guilds of one kind or another existed for many hundreds of years, they were truly important roughly between the twelfth and the fifteenth centuries. That period saw the growth of towns and town life in Europe, and the guilds were a product of the towns.

By the sixteenth century, the economic system was changing. The days of the small craftsmen were drawing to a close as merchants began to form themselves into companies and to invest large sums of money in businesses. Where one or two craftsmen had worked, large numbers of paid laborers took their place. In short, Europe was becoming a capitalist society.

Guilds could not fulfill their purpose in a capitalist system, and they began to decline. By the end of the eighteenth century, they had ceased to exist except as almost useless survivals from an age that had long passed. By that time, the Industrial Revolution was well under way: huge factories were springing up all over western Europe, and masses of laborers filled the grimy industrial cities. A new form of association was needed to care for the interests of the workers and, slowly, the trade union movement began to grow.

In the last hundred years, the trade unions have grown from tiny, persecuted groups into massive, powerful institutions. In some countries, they now exercise almost as much influence on the affairs of the nation as the guilds once exercised on the affairs of the town.

The early trade unionists looked back to the medieval guild as an example and an influence. Certainly, guilds and trade unions have many things in common, but while they are related, the trade unions are not the descendants of the guilds. Although the guild, like the trade union, looked after the interests of its

[3]

members, it did much more than that. The guild had duties toward all the townspeople and it was concerned with all parts of life (including religion), not just with work.

Although it is easy to find similarities — or differences — between the guild and the trade union there is one very important fact that makes all comparisons seem false: the society of medieval Europe, in which the guilds arose, was in almost every way entirely different from the society of the modern, industrialized world. People thought differently, spoke differently, acted differently, and even ate differently. To understand how the guilds worked, and why, we must first know something about the world in which the guildsmen lived.

THE RISE OF THE MERCHANTS

If we could fly in a helicopter over Europe as it was a thousand years ago, we would recognize few landmarks other than the hills and rivers. The first thing we would notice would be the wildness of the country. Hundreds of square miles would be uninhabited, and forests would cover the land where cities stand today. There would be no roads and few large towns. Europe was a land of small villages and, except for Rome, with its grand though dilapidated marble buildings, there was no town large enough to call a city.

Agriculture was the occupation of nearly all the people. Each village produced its own food and clothes and its own simple plows and tools. The few articles that it did not make could be bought from traveling tradesmen who displayed their wares weekly at the village market. The houses in the village were simply huts with wooden frames, mud walls, and thatched roofs. There were only two large buildings. One was the church and the other was the great house or castle of the local lord. The lord owned most of the land, and the surrounding forests were reserved for his hunting. He often "owned" most of the people as well, for the peasants who worked the fields were generally serfs, who were bound for life to work for their lord. They could never leave the village, and their children were born into the same life of serfdom.

At first glance, this system appears to be little better than slavery, but the lord had duties toward his serfs, as well as the other way round. Moreover, the serf, unlike a slave, took care of

A grain merchant (left) and a cloth merchant arranging a trade.

his own needs and provided his own food and clothing. The overlord had a right to only a portion of what his serfs produced. And despite the rules, it was sometimes possible to escape from serfdom.

One man who did escape was Saint Godric of Finchale. Godric was born into a family of poor peasants in northern England, in the year 1065. He was a wanderer, who did not like living in one place all the time. As a youth, he roamed along the coast, picking up goods that had been washed ashore from wrecked ships. With his pack on his back, he walked from one village to another, making a meager living from selling his finds. One day, he fell in with a party of merchants, and within a few years, he became a rich man.

Even during the worst times of the "Dark Ages," trade had never come to a complete stop in Europe. Goods were always exchanged between towns, and even between countries. But in Godric's time, trade was just beginning to expand after a long period of depression. Companies of merchants could be seen more often on the roads — or muddy tracks, as most of them were — between the larger towns.

Where did these merchants come from? No one can say for sure, but probably most of them began like Godric. It is difficult to discover the facts, because the men who wrote the history of the Middle Ages were nearly all priests or monks, who were not interested in such matters as trade or manufacturing. Indeed, the Church frowned on merchants. Making a profit was evil, said the Church, and some of these merchants were far too rich for the good of their souls.

The lords in their manor houses did not like the merchants either. Who were they, these dusty-footed travelers with their fine clothes and proud manners? They did not fit into the pattern of agricultural life: they were not serfs, but they were not lords either. Moreover, they were rich, and they had gained their riches in a way that the land-owning nobles could not understand and did not like.

The company that Godric belonged to bought goods where they were cheap and sold them where they were scarce (and therefore expensive). They joined together to load a ship and traded in Scandinavia and Belgium, as well as in England and Scotland. Godric himself, after he had made a large fortune, suddenly decided to give everything to the Church and to become a hermit. He was probably affected by the Church's teaching on profit-making, and felt that he was giving up a life of sin. Anyway, he became a holy man and, after his death, a saint.

Merchants did not earn their fortunes easily, for traveling in medieval Europe was extremely dangerous. The roads were so bad that carts could not be used in many places. Goods were carried on packhorses, and the merchants rode in formation around them, ready to fight off robbers. Shipping was even riskier. Apart from the threat of pirates, valuable cargoes were often lost through shipwreck.

Companies of merchants who joined together for reasons of safety and for making larger profits came to be called guilds. The word guild (or gild) is very old, and these were not the first examples of such associations or "brotherhoods." The tradesmen of ancient Rome belonged to similar organizations, called *collegia*. And at the time of the early merchant guilds, there were religious guilds, whose members joined together to worship and to perform acts of charity.

However, the rise of the merchant guilds was one of the most important developments in medieval society. It was closely connected with a process that had already begun during the eleventh century and is still going on today: the growth of towns and cities.

In medieval Europe many roads were so bad that not even carts could travel on them. Goods had to be transported by pack-horses.

Les fais des anciens doit
on voulentiers lyre ourr
et diligentement retenir
Car ilz peuent valoir et
donner bon exemple aux hardis en armes

Merchants did not spend all their days on the roads. They needed a home, a base from which they could run their business. Naturally, they began to congregate in the towns (or *burgs*), especially in those that stood on a river, on a coast, or on well-traveled crossroads.

The burgs were really more like fortresses than towns. They were quite small, and their most vital feature was the wall that surrounded them. In times of danger, the people from the nearby country could take shelter inside. The merchants settled just outside the walls, as there was little room for new buildings within. Their "new towns" or "suburbs" ("suburb" means "below the town") were bustling places, which soon became more lively and sometimes larger than the old towns. The merchants did not live there all by themselves. To carry on their business, they needed many kinds of goods and services. They needed porters for carrying their merchandise and sailors for their ships. They provided work for barrel-makers, rope- and sail-makers, wheelwrights and carpenters, as well as bakers, butchers, and sellers of vegetables.

Where did all these people come from? They could only come from the country, from the villages. Some of them were serfs, who had left their masters illegally. A serf who managed to stay in a town for more than a year without being caught became a free man and his master could no longer claim him. Workers and craftsmen from the country estates began to enter the towns in a steady stream, attracted by higher pay and better living conditions. Of course, the change was not sudden; society was not altered in a single moment. In fact this movement from the country to the towns went on for centuries.

An illustration from an old manuscript showing a street scene in medieval Europe.

[11]

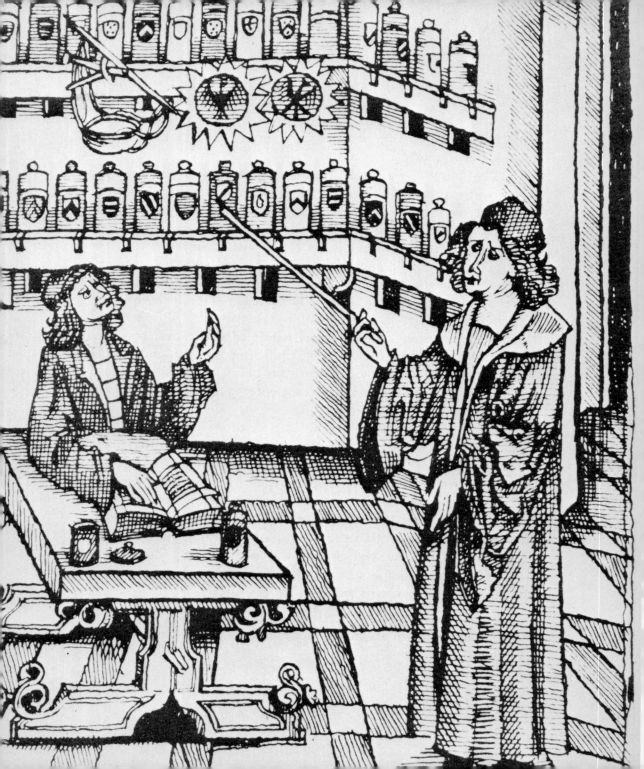

The growth of towns and cities began in northern Italy, then spread to Belgium, southern France, and eventually to Germany, England, and the rest of western Europe. It did not happen without causing disturbances. The nobles who held authority in the old towns did not know how to deal with the new class of men settled on their land. The conflict was especially sharp when the local lord happened to be a bishop (many medieval towns were ruled by bishops). The merchants were a threat to the bishop's authority, and the bishop disapproved of their way of life. But not all the local rulers were against the merchants, and the overlord, or king, was often on their side. National states as we know them had not yet developed: the French king, for example, ruled only a small region, and in most of France he had little authority. Nevertheless, the support of the overlord (whether he was a king, a count, or an emperor) was very useful to the new class of merchants when they were in conflict with the local ruler.

There were very few radicals or revolutionaries in the Middle Ages. No merchant wanted to overthrow the old system of government: merchants were not against serfdom; they were not against princes or bishops. But they did want their own freedom, at least the freedom to trade without restriction, and the local rulers were not all willing to grant them the liberty they demanded.

As time went by, the new, middle class of merchants began to gain control of the towns. Many of the old lords, who had formerly lived in the towns, sold their property to the merchants and moved out to the country.

The struggle between the new middle class and the old authorities went on for hundreds of years in some places. In

A physician ordering medicine from an apothecary.

[13]

Citizens of a commune receiving their charter.

one place, the middle class gained self-government easily; in another some sort of compromise was arranged. Most towns had long periods of peace, interrupted by fierce arguments or even civil war. But by the middle of the twelfth century, the signs were unmistakable. In all the more advanced areas of Europe, the old authorities were on the defensive. A few cities had become "communes" — republics in which all citizens voted. And everywhere, the new leaders of the towns were the richest and most powerful citizens, the merchants.

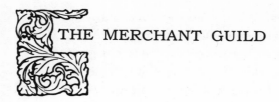

THE MERCHANT GUILD

Although we hear about a "class" of merchants and a "class" of craftsmen in medieval Europe, they were not always separate. Anyone who sold goods might be called a merchant. A man who made shoes was a craftsman, but if he also sold them in his shop (most shoemakers did) he could be called a merchant. A merchant generally was richer and more important than a craftsman, but some merchants were poor and some craftsmen were rich.

In the early days of the guilds, the borderline between merchants and craftsmen was vague. As time went by, the division between them became sharper.

We have seen how merchants first formed guilds for their own protection and profit and how the merchant guild became increasingly important with the growth of town life. The chief merchants were not only the leaders of the guild, but were also the leaders of the town government. In fact, in some towns, the merchant guild and the town government were one and the same.

The guild not only organized the trade and industry of the town, but also set up courts of justice, built streets and walls, and sometimes controlled the town's finances. It often received rights and privileges from the ruler. Guild members in the Flemish town of Saint-Omer during the eleventh century

A rich merchant (notice his fur-lined cloak) of the sixteenth century traveling with his goods to a foreign market.

enjoyed special treatment from the count of Flanders. They were excused from paying certain taxes and from military service. The count protected them from the power of the bishop of Saint-Omer, and allowed their animals to graze on fields that he owned.

During the thirteenth century, nearly every large town in France and England had a guild whose charter was granted by the king. Yet neither Paris nor London had a true merchant guild. Those cities were the capitals of their countries, and their lord was the king himself, not some bishop or baron. The king was eager to reduce the power of the bishops and nobles, who were his rivals, by granting special rights to the guilds, but in his own city he preferred to have no middle-class organization with extra powers. (However, the citizens of Paris and London managed to gain as many rights as the citizens of other towns.)

The poorer people in the towns, who made their living by working for a daily wage, did not have full citizenship. But everyone who was a full citizen belonged to the merchant guild. These early guilds were not restricted to men of one particular profession, as the craft guilds were later. They sometimes even included members of the nobility who owned land locally or had become involved in trade in the town.

The guilds were fairly democratic, and their officials were elected every year. But they were always dominated by the richer members. In their records, the same names appear again and again. The rich dealers in cloth (the most valuable item of trade in the Middle Ages) began to run the affairs of the town for their own profit. The smaller tradesmen were kept in their place by regulations that prevented them from growing richer. In some towns, wool could be bought only through the big merchants, who charged high prices. A weaver who bought his wool

Part of a painting of the procession of the guilds in Brussels in the sixteenth century.

elsewhere was fined by the guild, and the ordinary workers who were not members of the guild were treated even worse. The "blue-nails" (a rude name, which first applied to cloth workers but came to mean the whole working class) were not allowed to vote and had few rights.

During the thirteenth century, riots broke out in many European towns as the rich merchants steadily strengthened their hold on the towns. But by that time, the craft guilds had made their appearance everywhere. They were associations of men who practiced the same trade. The weavers were usually among the first to form their own guild, being more powerful and, it seems, more assertive than other craftsmen. The craft guilds were not, at first, the enemies of the merchant guilds. But they represented the future. The days of the great merchant guilds were coming to an end, and the craft guilds were taking over their position. The number of craftsmen was continually growing, while the number of merchants stayed about the same. The merchants who had become rich and powerful were beginning to replace the nobles as rivals to the king. Some of them had become large landowners. They could not always rely on the king to help them, as their ancestors had. In England, King Edward III passed a law in 1335 that allowed foreign merchants to trade freely in English towns. This was a blow to the merchant guilds and ended the monopoly they had enjoyed for so long. Their power began to decline.

By the end of the fourteenth century, the merchant guild in its old form had almost disappeared from most countries of western Europe. The selfish rule of the great merchants had helped to destroy it. Yet the merchant guild could boast of many successes. It had regulated trade and brought order and government to towns when there was no one else to do so. It had paved the roads and erected mills and bridges. And, of course, although the merchant guilds were dying, the great merchants themselves were not vanishing from the scene. On the contrary, they continued to play a leading role in the cities and towns of Europe, as their great houses and guildhalls in the old towns of Germany, Belgium, and other countries still testify.

THE CRAFT GUILD

In a medieval town, the tradesmen gathered in little colonies: bakers in one place, butchers in another, shoemakers somewhere else. Because the towns were so small, there were no "neighborhoods." A man could walk from the north gate to the south gate in a few minutes, and it was not necessary for shops to be scattered in different parts of the town. In Paris, a visitor walking across the bridge that led to the cathedral passed the drapers and skinners on his right. On the next street were the cloth workers and, next to them, the makers of gloves and shoes. If he walked in the other direction, he was among the butchers and poulterers and, on the opposite side of the road, the tanners of leather, the basket makers, and the bottlers. After a two-minute stroll he would pass the saddlers and the cabinet makers and come to the wheelwrights and the ironmongers.

Street names in the city of London remind us of the medieval town. Today's traffic, as it roars along Cheapside, passes streets with names like Wood Street, Milk Street, Bread Street, and Ironmonger's Lane, where once lived the sellers of wood, the milkmen, the bakers, and the ironmongers.

In the towns of Flanders (Belgium), which was the most advanced country in medieval Europe, craft guilds began as early as the eleventh century, perhaps earlier. Germany was not far behind, and soon the towns of every country in western Europe had craft guilds of some kind. At first, they were "un-

A medieval shop.

official" associations; but they quickly gained charters from the government, which made them legal. It was easier for the government to deal with a guild than with independent craftsmen, and for that reason governments were willing to recognize the existence of the craft guilds.

The governments of kings and princes were friendly — or at least neutral — toward the craft guilds. But the governments of the towns themselves were not so friendly. Town governments resented these groups of craftsmen who enjoyed special rights. In many towns, the early history of the craft guilds was a story of conflict. Sometimes the guild was on top; sometimes the town succeeded in suppressing it for a time. But in the end, the guilds survived.

The weavers were usually in the front of the battle — in Flanders especially, but also in other countries. The weavers were the strongest and best-organized of the craftsmen. Their trade, cloth-making, was the most prosperous trade in Europe, and because their goods were made for export, the weavers could put pressure on the rich merchants who were both the exporters of cloth and the leaders of the town government. Naturally, craftsmen like the butchers or the bakers, who worked for a small, local market, did not have as much influence.

In the German town of Cologne, a wool-weavers' guild existed before the year 1050, and within the next fifty years or so, we hear of weavers' guilds in Mainz, Speyer, Worms, and Frankfurt. Although the weavers of London received their charter during the reign of Henry I (1100–1135), that did not end their struggle for recognition. In fact, it marked the beginning of a long battle between the weavers' guild on the one hand and the mayor and citizens of London on the other.

Glassmakers at work.

The London weavers' charter gave the guild the right of self-government, which made it independent of the city government. The weavers even had their own court, and if a member of the guild was arrested for fraud, or debt, or for any small crime connected with his trade, he had the right to be tried in the court of the guild, not in the ordinary courts.

The weavers' privileges irritated the city authorities. During the reign of King John (1199–1216), the mayor and aldermen of the city persuaded the king to disband the guild. "The Guild of Weavers," said the king's proclamation, "shall not from henceforth be in the City of London, neither shall be at all maintained." How did the citizens persuade the king to ban the guild? It was very simple. In exchange for their privileges, the guild paid the king a "rent" of eighteen marks a year. But if the king would end the guild, the citizens promised to give him a gift of twenty marks a year!

The weavers, however, were not put down so easily, for during the next reign, their guild was back in business. Probably, King John's order had never been carried out, and perhaps the mayor of London had failed to produce the twenty marks. Anyway, in 1221 we find the city again at loggerheads with the weavers. This time, the royal government seems to have been on the weavers' side. An old chronicle relates that the guildsmen, "fearing lest the mayor and citizens of London should extort from them their charter," had delivered the precious document to the royal treasury for safekeeping.

A century later, the weavers were still fighting for their rights. In 1321, King Edward II's judges were inquiring into all organizations in the city that claimed special rights. That included the weavers' guild. The jury, all London citizens, were unfriendly to the weavers. Yet they had to admit that the weavers' charter, which by that time was two hundred years old,

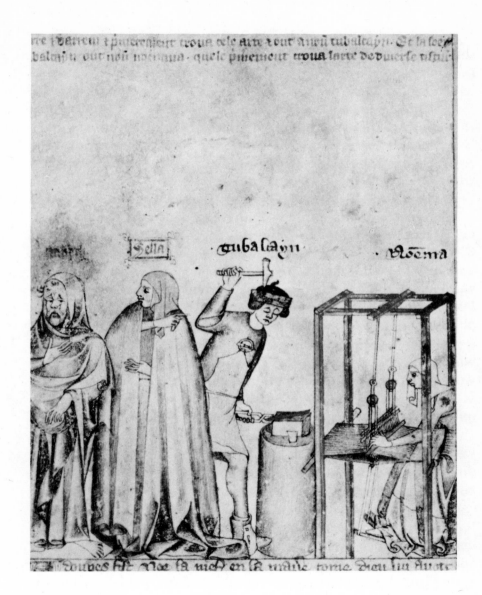

Weaving.

was legal and correct. Being honest men, they could not deny the clear rights of the weavers, though they did make their position clear by making some harsh remarks about the way in which the weavers exercised their rights.

What exactly were the rights of a craft guild? Of course they were different in different places and in different guilds. But the most important one, which they all possessed, was the right to control trade, as the weavers' guild of London controlled the weaving trade in that city.

Each guild was headed by a warden, or governor, who was either elected or appointed. The warden of the bakers' guild in Troyes was appointed by the local prince, the count of Champagne. In Rome, each guild had a cardinal as an overlord, and in cities that had a republican form of government, the wardens of the guilds were often city magistrates. In northern Italy, among other places, the warden was elected. The names of the candidates were put into a box and a child, or sometimes a priest, was asked to draw a name. A slightly different system was used by the butchers' guild of Arras, in Flanders. Balls of wax were placed in a jar, and each candidate drew one. On one of the balls, the names Jesus and Mary were written, and the man who drew it became the head of the guild.

The larger guilds had several other officials besides the warden. One of the great guilds of Florence had at least ten different posts, such as "treasurer" and "proctor," which had to be filled by election. The jobs were not popular, because they carried many duties with them and no pay. But no one served for more than a year, some only for a few months, and after his term of office was ended, a man could not be reelected until and agreed period of time had passed.

Most guilds were not so complicated and had fewer members. In a town of 20,000 people (a large town for those days)

Guild officials taking their oath of office.

there were not many dealers in pepper, for example, and the pepperers' guild would not have had more than ten or twelve members.

The craft guilds came into existence to protect the shopkeepers, small tradesmen, and craftsmen from the power of the rich merchants who ruled the town. Their first aim was an economic one: to protect their own businesses. And they did this, first, by looking after the welfare of their members and, second, by ensuring that their members were honest.

The guilds established strict rules for their members to follow, to make certain that all goods were of the correct standard. A dyer of cloth in Florence was told exactly what dyes he should use, what strength they had to be, and how many times the material should be dipped in the dye. It was almost like a religious ceremony. The guild of fishermen in Rome determined the size of the fishermen's nets, and the Roman fishmongers had to use scales with holes in them, so that they did not weigh any water along with the fish. A butcher in Maine, France, had to be able to prove that the meat he was selling came from an animal that had entered the town alive. If he could not produce two witnesses to say that they had seen the animal alive, he was in trouble.

For the most part these regulations were sensible and protected the customer as well as the honor of the guild. But some of the guild's rules were so strict that they seem rather silly. In Florence, the jewelers were not allowed to use imitation stones under any circumstances. It did not make any difference if the jeweler *said* they were imitations. Confusion might arise in the future, and the guild must never be suspected of fraud. A Paris goldsmith once made a gold-plated bowl. He did not intend to sell it as solid gold, but nonetheless, the guild forbade him to sell it at all and warned him not to make any more plated objects.

[30]

Armorers making helmets and a sword.

In some ways, the craft guild was like a large family. It tried to create a "brotherhood" of craftsmen, and to give all its members a fair chance. No one was allowed to profit at the expense of the others. Suppose a fresh supply of hides arrived in town. The whole lot might be bought by one tanner. But he was not allowed to use them all himself if another tanner needed some. Nor could he sell them to his fellow-tanners at a profit. Some guilds actually took charge of buying all raw material and then sold it to their members at a standard price. For example, all raw wool entering Florence was bought by the guild, which sold it to the wool-weavers at a set rate.

The members of the craft guild were not all equally rich, and the guild tried to prevent any member from becoming too rich or too poor. The number of workmen and apprentices who could be employed by one craftsman was limited by the guild. Often, it was not more than three or four. No member was allowed to lure a workman away from his employer by offering a higher wage.

Another common rule stated that work begun by one man could not be completed by another. This was an awkward rule for the doctors' guild in Florence, for it meant that a patient could not change doctors. No advertising was allowed, of course, and no "free samples" could be given.

The craft guild thus bound its members with many rules and regulations. What did the craftsman gain in return? Above all, he gained protection in his work. If he enjoyed reasonably good luck, the guild would save him from going bankrupt. It prevented competition, which might ruin him, by restricting the number of craftsmen in his trade and by preventing outsiders from establishing businesses in the town. If his trade suffered as a result of fire or robbery, or through his own illness, the guild helped him build it up again. Some guilds had hospitals for their members.

A member of a guild might enjoy rights that other citizens did not have. Perhaps he was excused from paying certain taxes or customs duty. If a man had wronged him, the guild would help him to be justly compensated. When business was bad, or the supply of raw materials had been cut off by war, many townspeople were in danger of starving. But the guild member was the last to suffer.

In the Middle Ages, the most powerful institution in Europe was the Christian Church. Religion ruled men's thoughts and actions, whether they were kings or bishops, priests or craftsmen. Many guilds employed a priest to conduct services for the members and say Mass for the dead. If a man died without leaving sufficient funds for his funeral, the guild paid for it. Four of his guild brothers carried the coffin, and all of them were expected to attend the ceremony. Those who did not had to have a good reason for their absence.

Many guilds had their own patron saint, and their own church. They paid for windows in cathedrals and altars in parish churches. In old city churches today, the coat of arms of a craft guild can often be seen among the memorials to kings and nobles.

The guild member was expected to be not only a good and honest tradesman, but also a good and honest *man*. The guild was concerned about its members' characters as well as their work. Wrongdoers could be punished, and in the Middle Ages punishment was severe. Cutting off a hand was a common way of discouraging thieves. Men who were guilty of less serious crimes had to pay a fine to the guild. The fine was often paid in goods rather than money. For failing to carry out some duty, a man might have to provide thirty gallons of wine for the next

guild feast. A French butcher, who sold some meat at an unfair price, had to pay a fine of a pig's carcass. The guild's worst punishment was expulsion. A man who was expelled from the guild could not practice his craft and had no way of earning a living.

As we have seen, many craft guilds began as illegal associations, and had to struggle to survive. The struggle between the London weavers and the city government was not unusual. Similar struggles took place in towns throughout western Europe. But by the fourteenth century, the craft guilds had won. They had become respectable. The more powerful guilds included great men among their members. No less a person than King Edward III of England was a member of the guild of linen-armorers.

The meeting of the guild was a serious affair. All the members attended, and the meeting could begin only when the chest that contained the guild's charter and other symbols of its power was unlocked in a solemn ceremony. Many guilds had their own uniform for these occasions. The guilds of London (which still exist) are called Livery Companies, and their livery (uniform) is still worn at ceremonies in the city of London.

The guilds liked to preserve an air of secrecy. No one was supposed to discuss the guild's business outside the guild meeting, and "trade secrets" were jealously concealed from possible rivals. Florentine craftsmen had a method for producing fine silver and gold brocade, which remained a closely guarded secret for many years. In Venice, a law of 1454 laid down terrible penalties for a citizen who took his craft to another state. If he

A French stained-glass window commemorating various crafts, including a fuller (top left) and a butcher (bottom left).

[35]

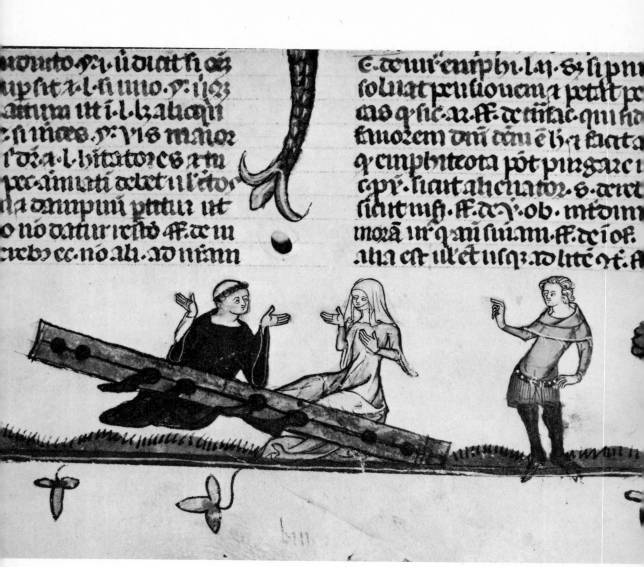

The stocks, a common form of punishment. The offenders this time are a friar and a young woman.

did not return when ordered, his relatives were to be thrown into jail. And if that did not bring him back, the law said that "secret measures will be taken to have him killed."

In England, another word for craft was "mystery," and a spirit of mystery often clung to medieval guilds. This spirit survives today in the society of freemasons. Freemasonry is a semisecret society, a charity that looks after its own members, and it exists throughout the world. Freemasons are supposed to have signs, like a special kind of handshake, by which they recognize each other. In the past, they had great influence in certain professions, and as a result they made many enemies. However, there is nothing sinister about freemasonry today, although Roman Catholics are still forbidden to join.

Freemasons trace their society back to the medieval guild of masons (builders). The masons were unusual among craftsmen because, unlike other trades, they did not stay in one place. They moved from one building site to the next. At each place they built a lean-to shed, called a lodge (the local branches of freemasons today are called lodges). The lodge was a workshop, an office, and a club, in fact a home away from home. Sometimes the masons worked on buildings far away from the towns — they built the great, lonely castles of medieval nobles — and they were bound together in the brotherhood of their trade even more closely than other craftsmen.

In the late Middle Ages, the separate guilds of masons began to join into larger guilds. All the masons' lodges in German-speaking Europe were brought together in the middle of the fifteenth century. There were three central lodges in Cologne, Zürich, and Vienna, and the "capital" was the lodge in Strasbourg — always a great city for masons because of the construction of its huge cathedral, which had been going on for two centuries.

[37]

Above: This painting of a religious subject — building the Tower of Babel — also shows methods of building at the end of the Middle Ages. Right: Sign of the butchers' guild of Saint Gall (Switzerland). The trademarks of members of the guild are shown around the sides.

Other guilds also formed unions. For instance, all the German cutlers, who made knives, gradually came under the guilds of four great cities. And the tailors of Silesia (now part of Poland and Czechoslovakia) made a united guild of twenty-five towns.

Unfortunately, the guilds quarreled more often than they cooperated. Europe during the late Middle Ages was still a continent of towns rather than nations. Neighboring cities were rivals, if not enemies. And the greater the city, the fiercer the rivalry. Ghent and Bruges, the richest cities of Flanders, were constantly bickering. So were Florence and her neighbor Pisa.

In much the same way, individual guilds often disagreed. Part of the trouble was that in many trades, more than one guild was involved. Wool passed through the hands of five or six different kinds of craftsmen before it became cloth. In some French towns, the sellers of wine were divided into five different classes: hotel-keepers who offered drinks, meals, and a bed; tavern-keepers, who served food and drink; bar-keepers, who served only drink; retailers, who sold wine in bottles to be taken away; and wholesale merchants, who supplied all the others. These classes could not always be kept separate. When a hotel-keeper sold a bottle of wine to a customer, he was stepping on the toes of the retailer. If a bar-keeper sold some cake that his wife had baked, he was trespassing on the rights of the tavern-keeper. Every such incident caused trouble — arguments, lawsuits, even fights. Trade-union quarrels over which man does what job are not new. The craft guilds knew all about such disputes.

 THE APPRENTICE

The guild member was called a "master" of his craft. He had his own shop where he produced and sold his goods. He lived above the shop with his family; he employed one or two workmen, or journeymen, and usually had at least one apprentice.

An apprentice is a young person who is learning a trade by working with an experienced craftsman. During the Middle Ages, virtually every master and every journeyman had been an apprentice in his time. In some countries, apprenticeship lasted for only two or three years, but it was usually longer. In England, most trades required an apprenticeship of seven years. During the sixteenth century the ancient guild of saddlers decreed that apprentice saddlers had to serve for at least ten years.

The apprentice started very young, often at ten or twelve years of age. When his parents found a master who was willing to take him, a legal contract was drawn up, which stated the conditions of his employment. Contracts were governed by the guild, and the guild ensured that both sides kept the agreement. The boy's parents paid an "entrance fee" to the master, and sometimes a yearly fee as well. It might be so many bags of flour, or a couple of sheep, or it might be a simple payment of cash. In return, the master promised to take the apprentice into his home and teach him his craft. He also fed him and bought his clothes; but he did not, as a rule, pay him any wages.

Of course, contracts were not the same in every country and every craft. In one place, the parents might agree to provide

gma. fastidium. & maciem sustinent.
Flebothomia quoq; incium est sa
pitatis. mrein sincerat. memoriam
pbet uesicam purgat. Cerebrum ex
siccat medullam calefacit auditum
apit lacrimas stringit fastidium
tollit stomaco pfiat. Digestionem
muitat sensum dirigit somnum
facit longiorem uita credit animi

uires. aut graces. sedm tempus. aut
mutationes caloris. Si sanguis e pn
apio exterit niger ufq; ad rufium co
lorem ueniat di autem spissus. aut
grassus fuerit uisq; ad tenuitatem
aquosam ueniat. H on tam diu cur
rat sanguis ut lyptusma fiat idest
lassitudo. uel debilitatio stomachi.

their son's clothes while he was an apprentice. In another place, the master might agree to pay a small wage after some time had passed. Some contracts laid down what rights the master had over his pupil. They were usually the same rights as a parent's. For instance, a master could punish his apprentice by beating him. A contract with a rope-maker in Florence contained a clause saying that the boy might be beaten — as long as no blood was drawn!

Cruel and mean masters did exist, undoubtedly, and the old records report some horrible incidents. More than one apprentice was beaten to death by his master. Many young men ran away to become beggars or thieves. When they did, their master had to keep a place open for a reasonable time in case they should return. But if they had not come back within a few months, the contract was ended.

The complaints of apprentices against their masters were investigated by the guild. The guild was especially interested in the apprentices' welfare, because they were the masters of the future. The number that could be employed by one master was strictly limited; usually not more than two were allowed. If a master had more, they would not be so well taught.

Once he had learned the basics of the craft, the apprentice was extremely valuable to his master because he worked for nothing. Therefore, masters would have liked to employ more apprentices. As that was not allowed, they found another way to profit from this supply of cheap labor. They steadily lengthened the time of apprenticeship, and so kept their unpaid workers for as long as possible.

Some apprentices were lucky enough to have good masters who treated them kindly. But many others must have had a

A physician instructing his apprentice.

[43]

miserable time. For years on end they had to work very hard — sixteen hours a day in the summer — without wages. They often had poor food and very little clothing. They might be cruelly beaten for the smallest fault.

Yet their life was much more pleasant than the life of young people of some later times. Working-class children in nineteenth-century Europe, or black children born into slavery in America, had to work harder and suffered more. And they could not hope for an easier life in the future. Medieval apprentices could at least look forward to better days.

By the sixteenth century, when the guilds were breaking down, the rules governing apprenticeship were not often obeyed. Governments were worried, and tried to take over control. In the England of Queen Elizabeth I, an act of Parliament called the Statute of Artificers in 1563 tried to enforce the apprentice system throughout the country. Every craftsman had to serve as an apprentice for seven years. By this act the government hoped to reduce the number of people roaming the country without any occupation. Young men, the Elizabethan government believed, could not be trusted to work steadily unless they were supervised. As the act said, "Until a man grow into 23 years, he for the most part, though not always, is wild, without judgment, and not of sufficient experience to govern himself." However, the act, like most rules for young people, was widely disobeyed.

A young mason and carpenter demonstrating their ability to the guild master.

 THE JOURNEYMAN

When a man had finished his apprenticeship, he became a skilled workman, called a journeyman. He might go on working for the same master, but he would receive wages. Every man who completed his apprenticeship became a journeyman. But not every journeyman became a master.

To become a full member of the guild, a man had to pay an entrance fee. In some guilds, the amount was too large for a journeyman to pay, and as time went by, fees went up. So there developed two kinds of journeymen: those who had recently been apprentices and hoped soon to become masters, and those who remained journeymen all their lives.

In every town, the journeymen who needed jobs gathered early in the morning at some central place, like the market square. A master seeking to hire help went there to find it. Local workmen had the first chance, and foreigners could only be hired when the natives were all employed.

The master and the journeyman then made a contract. It was not a written contract because, quite possibly, neither man could read or write. All the same, it was a binding agreement. The journeyman swore an oath on the Bible to obey the terms of the contract. He had to prove, not only that he was a good workman, but also that he was a man of good moral character. He would be living and working all day in the master's shop, and probably eating with the master's family. Naturally, the master wanted to know that the journeyman would neither steal his goods nor run off with his daughter.

Journeymen carpenters making a rafter.

A gathering of workmen with their tools.

Journeymen usually worked for one master for only a short time: it might be a year, it might be a few weeks, or it might be a day or two. Most small craftsmen could not afford to pay a workman over a long period, which included times when business was slack. The guild fixed the local wage rate, so the journeyman could not be cheated by a stingy master. On the other hand, wages were generally low. They varied from place to place — workmen in Flanders, for example, were paid better than others — and they were often paid in goods as well as money. A sheep for two weeks' work was a fair wage in the early fourteenth century.

A journeyman also received his food for nothing, and as he ate with the master, he usually ate fairly well. He lived in rented rooms, and he had few possessions other than the clothes that he wore. It was extremely difficult for him to marry and have children.

In the early years of the craft guilds, there was no sharp division between the three kinds of craftsmen. Masters, journeymen, and apprentices were all "brothers." Although the journeymen were not full members of the guild, the guild looked after them as well as the masters. By the end of the fourteenth century, this was changing. A gap had opened between the masters and their men. In the richer guilds, those that produced goods for export, the masters were great merchants who had become more like nobles than tradesmen. Even among poorer crafts, like the grocers or fishmongers, the master was often a well-to-do city father, while the journeyman was a poor worker.

In some trades, especially the cloth trade, the old system of master and workmen in a private shop had disappeared. Instead, the master hired men and women to work in their own homes. Under this system, he could hire many more workers.

But the old family spirit of the craftsman's shop had gone, and with every passing year, it became harder for the journeyman to improve his position. In many towns, dissatisfied workmen rebelled in protest against low wages and poor working conditions. As the guilds had failed to help them, the journeymen began to form their own fraternities.

Some guilds, especially grand ones like the London Livery Companies, already contained a kind of subguild for journeymen, called a company of bachelors. The bachelors were not allowed to wear the livery, and they possessed fewer rights than the masters of the company. Journeymen's fraternities that were not ruled by the guild were illegal. Every country passed laws against them, but it was never easy to enforce unpopular laws in the Middle Ages, and the journeymen continued to organize their own fraternities.

These fraternities of wage-earning workmen were more like our trade unions than were the guilds. The old records tell of demands for higher pay and of strikes against the employers. However, medieval men had no idea of the "rights of labor." The labor movement really began in the nineteenth century, and medieval workers would not have understood the ideas behind it.

Toward the middle of the fourteenth century, an outbreak of plague called the Black Death swept through Europe and killed approximately one-third of the population. One result was that labor became scarce. Employers were willing to pay much higher wages to get workers. In some places, journeymen did well for a time. But only for a short time. Governments hastily stepped in to prevent this dangerous inflation. It became illegal to pay, or receive, wages at a higher rate than the rate that had existed before the Black Death.

As national governments increased their control of industry, the ordinary workers became weaker (see final chapter). During the sixteenth century, the old guild rules, which had often worked for the good of the journeyman, were worn away. Workers moved about more easily from place to place, and wage rates could be kept down by importing foreign labor. In England, there were fewer strikes of workmen during the seventeenth century than there were during the fourteenth century — not because workers were happier, but because they had less power.

 THE BAKER

We have already seen how some merchants and craftsmen in the Middle Ages became much richer than others. Some trades were more profitable, and some men were more successful. In this chapter and the next, we shall look at the lives of two very different guild members, a French baker in the fourteenth century and an English wool merchant in the fifteenth century. Both Giles the Baker and William Bates the merchant are imaginary characters. They did not really exist, although they might have.

Giles the Baker lives in a town in northern France. He is about thirty-five years old and he has a wife and two small children, the survivors of a family of four. Perhaps he was unlucky to lose two babies, but he would have thought God was amazingly good to him if all four had lived.

The sun has hardly risen above the roofs when Giles heaves himself out of bed, while his wife and children sleep. Over the shirt that he wears night and day, Giles pulls a heavy, woolen smock with wide sleeves. A cock is standing in the street outside, crowing noisily. Giles opens the wooden shutter and looks out, but a cold wind blows through the glassless window and he quickly shuts it again. He shuffles downstairs, pausing at the bottom to give a gentle kick to his apprentice, who sleeps at the back of the shop.

There is a bag of grain to be taken to the miller, who will grind it into flour. Giles wonders if the boy can be trusted with

snelement li fu li haubers desuestus

biau fiex ou est mes nies que est il deuenus

florent li respondi qme homme trascus

ie ne sai ou il est si ait mame salus

n lui ne lamiral nai ie encore veus

p le mien escient vous les aues pdus

a lioz les vous a en bataille tollus

es tost loz en doit estre le guerredon rendus

quant danclins ifu pris z trestout retenus

quant du fil alixand fu tost secoureus

A baker's shop, from an old manuscript.

this errand. Although he has been with Giles for two years, he is not yet fifteen, and the miller has been known to cheat his customers. Ten pounds of grain may go into the mill, but the customer may collect the flour made from only nine pounds. That miller, with his silk hose and his new cart, is looking suspiciously prosperous these days.

The street is stirring. Standing at the front of his shop, Giles calls out greetings to his neighbors. A monk goes by, his face invisible under his hooded cloak. Giles watches him pass, but says nothing. He does not care for monks. Despite their holy vows, too many of them are fond of money and pretty women.

Giles is looking out for his journeyman-baker, who is late for work as usual. But here he comes now, swinging the leg that is half-crippled as the result of a childhood disease. That bad leg is sometimes useful. It explains why the man is late this morning, and why he must leave well before dusk, to get home before the thieves start taking their places in the dark streets. The man is a good worker, though. Giles knew that when he hired him, for last year he worked for Giles's friend Pierre, whose bakery is only a few doors down the street.

The journeyman's first job today is to clean out one of the ovens. After a time, the big stone ovens get covered with soot, which has to be scraped off with a wooden paddle, so that it will not fall on the baking bread. Giles helps him with this task, then prepares the dough for the morning's baking. He wipes his hands on his apron first because, although he has never heard of germs or infection, he does not want his sooty hands to turn the dough gray.

It is Friday, usually a busy day. Although the shop will

A medieval mill.

[55]

be open on Saturday morning, it will close before midday in preparation for the Sabbath. Giles may not like monks, or priests for that matter, but he loves — perhaps fears is a better word — the Christian God. He understands very little of the services in church because he knows no Latin. But he would not think of missing Mass.

Bakers do not often grow very rich, and Giles is a poor craftsman by comparison with some others in the town. One of his troubles is that many people bake their own bread, instead of buying it from Giles and his fellow-bakers. However, business is not too bad. This customer coming in now, for instance, is the wife of a saddle-maker who lives on the next street. When Giles was an apprentice, she baked bread in her own kitchen, but since her husband became warden of the saddlers, she has taken to buying it. Of course she is old, must be fifty at least, though she would look younger if her face was not so badly marked by the scars of smallpox.

Giles has been working for two or three hours before he has his breakfast — a piece of his own bread washed down with cheap wine. His apprentice is not back yet from the mill, and if he does not get back soon, he may miss his breakfast and get a blow from Giles instead.

The main meal is eaten in the early afternoon. Today they will all sit down to a pike, baked by Giles's wife and served with strong-flavored herbs. Giles's household is rich enough to eat meat fairly often, though not every day. Poorer people make their main meal on vegetable stew, but everyone prefers to eat meat when he can afford it. At the feast of the guild the menu is beef, pork, chicken, partridge, and goose — no vegetables, just a splendid array of meat and game.

The guild's feasts are the most enjoyable entertainment in Giles's life. His wife goes with him and they both eat and

ou quel nous auons baille aut du regime domestique selon me
saence par laide de celui dont toute saence et boute bient.
¶ Par fine le second liure du regime des princes ou quel est traite
du gouuernement de maison. Et comance le tiers liure le quel traite
du regime de ate et comuline. Dont le premier chapitre declaire
que la comunite de ate est ancienemet principale et est constituee
pour cause de bien.

*Above: Shops open for business in a French town during the
fifteenth century. Over: Brueghel's painting of a village wedding
(complete with bagpipes) gives us an idea of the atmosphere at
a feast for ordinary folk.*

drink a little more than is good for them. Giles has been known to throw a crust of bread at his friend Pierre and hit him in the ear. It was no coincidence that Pierre happened to stumble, later on, while holding a jug of wine near Giles's head.

But at the business meeting of the guild, everyone is solemn. All the master-bakers are there, and prayers are said before the meeting begins. The charter of the guild lies on the table before the warden. It is an important document, for the livelihood of the bakers depends on it.

In peaceful times, nothing very unusual happens at guild meetings. There may be complaints to be investigated. Perhaps a journeyman has accused his master of making him work extra long hours. The master admits it, but explains that his work had been delayed by the failure of the morning's baking. Still, the guild's rules must be obeyed, and the master is lucky to escape without a fine.

In his bakery, Giles ends the day's work as the light is beginning to fade. His journeyman has already limped off to his lodgings on the other side of the town. His apprentice is yawning and, although it is only eight o'clock, Giles too is ready for bed. He sits in his shop listening to the daytime sounds growing faint, picking his teeth with a wooden stick. It has been a peaceful day, and that, to a medieval townsman, is a good day. Giles is content.

His world is a small one. He has never traveled more than a few miles from his town, and seldom goes beyond the walls. He knows little about the rest of the world, and what he does know is a mixture of facts and fantasy that he has collected from sermons in church and from the talk of travelers whom he has met in the inn. But although Giles leads a simple life and has had no real education, he is an intelligent man. As a rule, he believes what he is told, but he knows that the world is not a simple place. Sometimes he feels he would like an answer to the questions that drift into his mind. But he does not have much time to spend thinking. He looks round his shop, makes sure the door is barred, and climbs the stone steps to his bed.

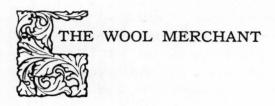 THE WOOL MERCHANT

In the last chapter we looked at one day in the life of an imaginary fourteenth-century French baker. In this chapter, we shall look at a year in the life of a different sort of tradesman, an English wool merchant of the fifteenth century.

Giles was concerned with the affairs of his own small town. But William Bates is involved in business that takes him to France and the Low Countries as well as all over England. He is one of the richest merchants in England.

The cloth trade is by far the largest business in Europe in William Bates's time. The great cloth-making centers are in the Low Countries, especially Flanders, and in northern Italy. Sheep are raised everywhere, but English wool is the best. The cloth-making towns of Flanders buy nearly all their wool from English merchants. William Bates's coat is of English wool, but it was made in Flanders. However, the English themselves are beginning to rival the Flemish weavers. After all, if the Flemings make cloth out of English wool, why should the English not make their own cloth? But William Bates belongs to an older merchant tradition: he exports raw wool to the continent. The new, fast-growing English industry is not a favorite of his, because it threatens to put his customers out of business.

William Bates is a fellow of the Company of the Merchants of the Staple. The Staple is a town that the government has appointed as the center of the wool trade. During the fifteenth century, it is the port of Calais (an English possession then although, of course, Calais is in France). All wool (and other

The house of a rich English wool merchant.

goods too) has to pass through the Staple, a system which makes the collection of customs dues a simpler task than it would be if the trade was conducted through a hundred different ports.

William Bates owns a large house in a village near London and an office in the city itself. Although he employs agents to carry on much of his business, he is often away from home himself. In the spring he rides out to the West Country, a journey of nearly a hundred miles, to buy his wool. Other merchants are riding to the north and the east at the same time, but Bates prefers the West Country wool. He has been coming here for many years, and buys from dealers whom he knows to be honest. He meets many old friends and fellow-merchants, but he is sorry to see buyers from Flanders and Italy there. They are rivals, for the wool that they buy does not pass through the English Staple in Calais.

Having finished his business, Bates returns to London, traveling with a group of companions for safety against robbers. His wool will be packed by officials who are appointed by the Staple. They seal the bales so that no one can interfere with them before they are sold. Strict rules govern the packing and grading of wool. No earth, sand, or hair must be mixed with it, and all the wool in each bale must be of the same standard (some merchants try to sell poor-quality wool by putting it in the middle of a bale and wrapping better-grade wool around the outside).

Packhorses carry the wool to the ports, and there William Bates has agents waiting to see that his goods are safe. Ships laden with goods sail from London or one of many other ports. This is the riskiest part of the business, for although the English Channel is less than thirty miles across, storms, enemies, and pirates wait in the narrow seas. In London, William Bates

The scene at a medieval cloth market.

breathes a sigh of relief when he hears that his wool has reached Calais safely.

Sometimes, Bates goes to Calais himself. He stays in a house licensed by the Company of the Staple to lodge its members as paying guests. At dinner, he sits at the high table with the prosperous merchants who have been his friends for many years, while less important men sit at smaller tables. There are only about three hundred merchants of the Staple, and William Bates knows most of them by name.

When the wool arrives in Calais, it is inspected by royal officers. Bates is in a little trouble this year because he knows that pack number seventeen, which the royal officers have chosen to inspect, contains substandard wool. However, he manages to change the label with pack number four, which is good wool, before the inspector arrives. A successful merchant always knows a few tricks, and if his customers complain that he has sold them second-rate goods, he will just shrug his shoulders.

With good luck, William Bates will sell all his wool in Calais soon after it arrives. But more likely, some will be held in the Staple's warehouses for several months. If it is not sold in a year, it becomes "old wool," but the Staple rules that the Flemish merchants must buy one lot of old wool with every three lots of new wool. Thus, all the wool is sold eventually.

From Calais, the merchant rides toward the cities of the Low Countries — Antwerp and Bruges, Ypres and Ghent. At each season of the year there is a great fair, or "mart," in Flanders, where merchants from every country of western Europe can be found. Besides selling wool, William Bates is looking for goods to buy. He selects some silk from the stall of a merchant from Genoa. He buys Flemish gloves for his wife, a

Money changing, a risky business even nowadays.

[66]

hat of beaver fur for himself, and some barrels of wine for his cellar.

He must also go to Flanders to collect his debts. The Flemish merchants buy their wool on credit, and William Bates needs his money in order to pay the wool-dealers in England. It is a complicated business and Bates must keep his wits about him, for the money may be paid in the coins of ten or twenty different states. The value of money depends on how much gold the coins contain, so a Flemish shilling is not necessarily the same value as an English shilling. Last year, he accepted some Venetian coins without knowing that the copper content had been increased and their value had therefore gone down. The Staple issues a list giving the value of all kinds of money, but it is not always up-to-date. William Bates's accounts are as complicated as those of any modern stockbroker.

And so from Flanders, William Bates sails again for London. Later in the year he is in Calais again, then in Flanders for the winter fair, the "Cold Mart" as it is called. And wherever he goes, the Company of the Staple governs his affairs. It gives him food and shelter when he is abroad; it watches over the quality of his wool; and it makes rules for buying and selling. If he becomes involved in a business quarrel, he can seek a judgment in the company's court. He pays his dues to the company, which in turn pays the duties owed to the king.

But the Company of the Staple is not quite a guild in the old sense. William Bates is a businessman in a society that is entering the age of capitalism. The strictly controlled guilds are disappearing, and Master Bates himself is a member of the London Grocers' Company, and, strangely, the Fishmongers' Company too. For these great livery companies are becoming clubs for the richer merchants rather than guilds of tradesmen. The great age of the guilds is drawing to a close.

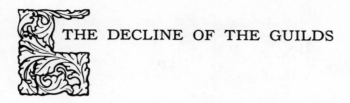 THE DECLINE OF THE GUILDS

In many countries, guilds still existed at the end of the eighteenth century, and a few still exist today. But they are lifeless skeletons compared with the guilds of the late Middle Ages. By the middle of the sixteenth century, the guilds were in decline. Why?

In the first place, society was changing: the old order was disappearing and in the vigorous new world of the Renaissance, developments hostile to the guilds were taking place. Europe was becoming a continent of national states, ruled by powerful monarchs. A man who had once owed his loyalty to his lord — the baron in the castle above the town — now began to feel that he was not just "Baron X's man," he was an "Englishman" (or a Frenchman, or a Spaniard), and his first loyalty was to his king. Even in countries like Germany and Italy, where no national state had yet appeared, political boundaries expanded as small provinces and towns were absorbed by larger ones.

A result of the growing importance of national states was the decline of the medieval town. The towns ceased to be isolated communities, busy with their own affairs and not much concerned with what was happening in other places. Capital cities like London and Paris became greater, but other cities lost their old independence. Trade, no longer confined within one town and the country around it, spread to take in the whole province and the whole state.

Under the old town economy, the guilds had made the rules for each town. But in the new economy of the province or

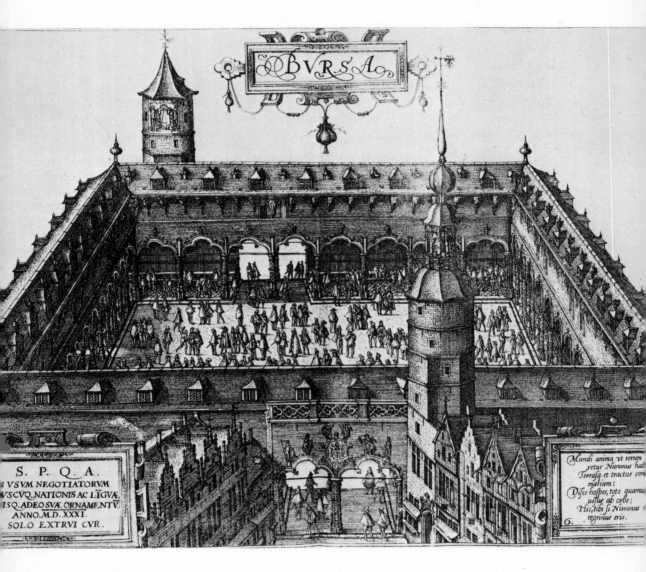

The exchange at Antwerp in the sixteenth century, when it was the greatest commercial center in the world.

the state, it was very inconvenient to have each town operating under its own rules. A new kind of authority was needed, which would supply the rules for trade and industry in the larger economic units that had replaced the towns. Who was to be the new authority? The answer could only be — the king. The matters that had once been decided by the guilds — prices, wage-rates, etc. — were now the subject of laws made by the royal government, which applied to the whole country. The English Statute of Artificers (see page 45) was an example of such a law. Besides ruling on the length of apprenticeships, it also tried to set prices and wage rates for the entire nation.

Although kings were not the enemies of the guilds, and had indeed found them to be useful allies against the power of local nobles, by the sixteenth century this alliance was becoming less valuable. The power of the king having increased, he no longer had so much to fear from his "overmighty" subjects.

As long as the guilds served a useful purpose in matters like tax collection and local government, the king did not interfere. The royal government, however, naturally wanted to improve the economy of his country, and the guilds were often obstacles in the way. They were not concerned with the national economy, only with their own trades and their own towns. The efforts of the king to build up the national economy sometimes clashed with the interests of the guilds. For example, kings were willing to admit foreign workers, which the guilds had tried to prevent. Henry IV of France wanted to start a silk industry in his country, so he planted mulberry trees and hired Italian workers from Genoa and other silk-producing districts. No doubt this was a good development for France, but it was resented by those guilds that feared competition from the new industry.

The guild system existed in a society where the population increased very slowly, if at all. The amount of goods bought and sold did not change much from year to year. The guilds, therefore, had good reason for restricting the number of men employed in each craft and for maintaining old methods of production. By the sixteenth century, the drawbacks of this system outweighed its advantages. Trade in Europe was expanding, and new markets were being opened in other lands as a result of the voyages of the explorers. To supply the growing trade, more goods were required. The old methods of production would not do.

Western Europe was entering the age of capitalism. The old master craftsman, with his little shop and his two or three assistants, was slowly forced out of business. The first "factories" appeared in the cloth trade; merchants bought ten or twenty looms, set them up in a large room, and hired workers to run them. Others sent the work out to men and women in their own cottages, and paid them according to the amount of work they completed.

Increasing trade required increasing investment. Merchants often joined together to hire a ship (for example), dividing the cost according to the quantity of goods that each man shipped. From there it was not such a large step to the founding of a business company, which hired the ship and owned the goods, while the merchants took a share of the company's profits. Although such companies at first seemed most useful for international trade, there was nothing to prevent any business from being organized in the same way.

In their day the craft guilds had many real merits. They controlled the standard of goods for sale and prevented dishonesty. But, right from the start, the craft guilds had many faults. Perhaps the chief trouble was that they were so conservative. We have seen many examples of how the strict rules of the guilds blocked progress. A craftsman had to obey the

[72]

rules, he had to follow the old customs. It was pointless to invent a better method of doing a job, because he would not be allowed to use it. Not only did this attitude prevent economic progress, it also dulled the talents of the craftsman. There was no motive for experimenting; there was no reason for producing more or better-quality goods. The craftsman could only go on making the same old things in the same old way, and if he had any special skill, it was probably wasted.

However, the guild gave him some security. Without it, his life would have been poorer and more dangerous. For its members, the guild was a very helpful institution. But for those who were not members, it was at best a nuisance and at worst a menace. This exclusive character of the guilds was another obstacle in the way of progress.

At the same time as the guilds were being threatened by the changes in European society, they were also rotting away from within. Like most human institutions, the guilds had never worked quite as well as they should have. There were always dishonest merchants, corrupt officials, cruel masters, and bad workmen. As time passed, the guilds did not get better; they got worse.

In their early years, the guilds helped to bring some democracy to life in the towns; masters, journeymen, and even apprentices were often all members of the guild; few masters were very rich, and few journeymen were very poor. But as time went by, some craftsmen became richer, and some workmen become poorer; employers and workers became two distinct classes. The guilds fell under the control of a group of the richest masters.

Journeymen found it more and more difficult to become masters. The entrance fee for becoming a master was steadily raised. Many crafts demanded an extremely elaborate "masterpiece," which few journeymen had time to make (a masterpiece

Trademarks of medieval wool merchants.

was an example of the craft — a clock for clockmakers, a saddle for saddlers, etc., that had to be presented by a man who wished to become a master).

However, if the new entrant happened to be the son of one of the masters, these steep entrance requirements were put aside. Such a man could often become a master without being a journeyman first, and in some places he did not even have to serve an apprenticeship. In this way, the masters (or a small group of them) kept control of the guild in their own hands and passed their power to their sons. The guild came under the rule of one or two great families.

At the same time, journeymen were getting poorer. During the sixteenth century, Europe went through a period of sharply rising prices — what we would call inflation. Wages went up also, but not as quickly as prices. In England, for example, wages increased by about one-third between 1485 and 1600. During the same period, the price of bread increased nearly five times. In other words, a man who earned three dollars in 1485 earned four dollars in 1600. But if he could buy (say) sixty pounds of bread with his wages in 1485, he could buy less than twenty pounds in 1600.

The guilds steadily lost their ability to control the quality of their goods: it was not difficult for a William Bates to cheat the inspectors at Calais by changing the labels on his wool. They wasted their time and energies fighting with each other: the wine merchants of Paris were involved in a lawsuit that lasted for 150 years. They became organizations for protecting the profits of the few men at the top, and the old rules were constantly broken.

The guilds stood in the way of economic progress, and therefore they were destroyed. Because they had become corrupt, no doubt they deserved to be destroyed. In the new age,

trade and industry grew so rapidly that a medieval craftsman would have been astonished by the changes in the towns of modern Europe. But something valuable was lost with the failure of the guilds. From the sixteenth to the nineteenth century, the gulf between employer and laborer steadily widened. Few medieval workmen ever lived in such dreadful conditions as the workers in the factories and mills of the nineteenth century. The guilds, at the outset anyway, stood for good workmanship, fair prices, and honest dealing. In the sixteenth century, men often lost sight of those principles. The doctrine of the "fair price" was forgotten. A new motto took its place — CAVEAT EMPTOR, "let the buyer beware!" Profit became king and reigns over us still.

Thaxted guildhall, England, one of many pleasant remains of the great days of the guilds in old towns of Europe.

BIBLIOGRAPHY

Ashley, William. *An Introduction to English Economic History and Theory*. New York: Kelley, 2 vols. in 1. Reprint of Pt. 1, 1888 and Pt. 2, 1893.

Bagley, John J. *Life in Medieval England*. New York: Putnam, 1960.

Brentano, Lujo. *On the History and Development of Guilds and the Origin of Trade Unions*. New York: B. Franklin, 1969.

Green, Alice S. *Town Life in the Fifteenth Century*. 2 vols. New York: Blom, 1907.

Gross, Charles. *The Guild Merchant: A Contribution to British Municipal History*. 2 vols. London: Oxford University Press, 1890.

Kendall, Paul M. *The Yorkist Age: Daily Life During the Wars of the Roses*. New York: Norton, 1970.

Pirenne, Henri. *Medieval Cities*. Gloucester, Mass.: Peter Smith, 1925.

————. *Economic and Social History of Medieval Europe*. New York: Harcourt Brace Jovanovich, 1936.

Power, Eileen. *Medieval People*. Gloucester, Mass.: Peter Smith, 1963.

Renard, Georges. *Guilds in the Middle Ages*. New York: Kelley, 1969 (reprint of 1918 ed.).

Thompson, James W. *Economic and Social History of Europe in the Later Middle Ages*. New York: Ungar, 1960 (reprint of 1931 ed.).

Thrupp, Sylvia L. *The Merchant Class of Medieval London.* Ann
    Arbor: University of Michigan Press, 1962.
Unwin, George. *Guilds and Companies of London.* 4th ed. New
    York: Barnes and Noble, 1964.

INDEX

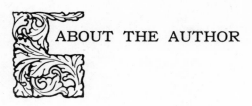# ABOUT THE AUTHOR

Neil Grant is a full-time writer who lives in a London suburb in his native England. Soon after receiving his master's degree in history from Cambridge University, Mr. Grant moved to the United States, where he worked for a number of years, first as a teacher but mostly as an editor for an encyclopedia. *Guilds* (A First Book) is his seventh book for young people published by Franklin Watts, Inc. His other titles are: *Benjamin Disraeli*, *Charles V, Victoria: Queen and Empress, The Renaissance* (A First Book), *Munich: 1938,* and *Cathedrals* (A First Book).